# COINS 4

## The Easy Way to Solve Math Word Problems

Solving math word problems can be challenging for many students. The **COINS** strategy makes this process easy! To use this strategy, students should perform the following steps:

Read the problem, then:

**C**ircle: Circle the key words and relevant information.

**O**peration: Write the operation (+, –, etc).

**I**nformation: Write the relevant information.

**N**umber Sentence: Write the math number sentence.

**S**olution Sentence: Write the solution as a complete sentence.

Students can use this strategy for just about any word problem they encounter. This book is broken down into the following sections:

Section 1: Adding Fractions

Section 2: Subtracting Fractions

Section 3: Adding & Subtracting Fractions

Section 4: Multiplying Fractions

Section 5: Dividing Fractions

Section 6: Multiplying & Dividing Fractions

Section 7: Multiplying & Dividing Whole Numbers

# Have fun!

# COINS 4 – Section 1
## Using COINS to Solve Fraction Word Problems
## Adding Fractions

When you read a word problem, certain <u>key words</u> can help you solve the problem.

---

### Fraction word problems

*Remember the following key words for adding fractions:*

**Addition**

- add
- altogether
- in all
- sum
- combined
- in total

---

When you solve word problems using **COINS**, remember to read the problem, then solve it as follows:

**C**ircle: <u>Circle the key words and relevant information (and cross out any irrelevant information)</u>.

**O**peration: : <u>**X**</u>, <u>÷</u>, etc.

**I**nformation: <u>Write the relevant information</u>.

**N**umber Sentence: <u>Write the math problem</u>.

**S**olution Sentence: <u>Write the solution as a full sentence</u>.

# Complete the Problems

Use **COINS** to solve these fraction word problems. Remember to circle the key words, draw pictures if necessary, and cross out any extra information. Then complete the steps using **COINS Strategy** .

**1.** Claire poured ⅖ of a cup of apple juice for her son and ⅘ of a cup of milk for her daughter. How much liquid did she pour in all?

❏ Circle key words.

Operation: _____

Information: _____

_____

Number Sentence: _____

Solution Sentence: _____

_____

| work space |
| --- |
|  |

**2.** Jake ate 1 ¼ bars of chocolate and Jane ate 1 ⅜ bars of chocolate. How much chocolate did they eat altogether?

❏ Circle key words & relevant information.

Operation: _____

Information: _____

_____

Number Sentence: _____

Solution Sentence: _____

_____

| work space |
| --- |
|  |

**3.** Annie spent ¼ of her money in one shop and ⅜ of her money in another shop. What fraction of her money did she spend?

❑ Circle key words & relevant information.

Operation: _____

Information: _____

_____

Number Sentence: _____

Solution Sentence: _____

_____

work space

**4.** A brownie weighs ⅚ ounces and a cookie weighs 4/9 oz. What is the total weight of 2 brownies and one cookie?

❑ Circle key words & relevant information.

Operation: _____

Information: _____

_____

Number Sentence: _____

Solution Sentence: _____

_____

work space

**5.** Amy ran $\frac{2}{5}$ of a mile on Monday, $\frac{5}{9}$ of a mile on Tuesday, and $\frac{6}{7}$ of a mile on Wednesday. How many miles did she run in all?

❏ Circle key words & relevant information.

Operation: _____

Information: _____

_____

Number Sentence: _____

Solution Sentence: _____

_____

_____

work space

**6.** Katrina donated $5\frac{7}{9}$ pounds of clothes to charity in January. In February she donated $4\frac{5}{9}$ pounds of clothes. What is the total weight of clothes she donated altogether?

❏ Circle key words & relevant information.

Operation: _____

Information: _____

_____

Number Sentence: _____

Solution Sentence: _____

_____

work space

**7.** Hallie went trick or treating on Halloween. At 5:00 PM she had $\frac{5}{6}$ pounds of candy. When she finished trick or treating at 8:00 PM she had received another $1\frac{4}{5}$ pounds of candy. How much candy did she receive in all?

☐ Circle key words & relevant information.

Operation: _____

Information: _____

_____

Number Sentence: _____

Solution Sentence: _____

_____

work space

**8.** Angel collects marbles. At the start of her collection her marbles weighed $1\frac{6}{9}$ ounces. She has since collected more marbles weighing $12\frac{3}{4}$ ounces. What does her collection of marbles now weigh altogether?

☐ Circle key words & relevant information.

Operation: _____

Information: _____

_____

Number Sentence: _____

Solution Sentence: _____

_____

work space

**9.** There were 92 ¾ pitchers of lemonade at a block party. Seven families then brought $^{62}\!/_5$ pitchers of lemonade. How much lemonade was at the block party altogether?

☐ Circle key words & relevant information.

Operation: _____

Information: _____

_____

Number Sentence: _____

Solution Sentence: _____

_____

work space

**10.** Aaron spent $^5\!/_6$ of an hour jogging and ¾ of an hour swimming. How much time did he spend exercising altogether?

☐ Circle key words & relevant information.

Operation: _____

Information: _____

_____

Number Sentence: _____

Solution Sentence: _____

_____

work space

**11.** Mary is trying to beat her sprinting record to see how far she can run in a minute. In March, her personal record was $\frac{2}{3}$ of a lap in a minute. In June her record improved by $\frac{1}{15}$ of a lap and it further improved by $\frac{1}{12}$ of a lap in August. What is her final best record?

❑ Circle key words & relevant information.

Operation: _____

Information: _____

_____

Number Sentence: _____

Solution Sentence: _____

_____

work space

**12.** Mrs. Casey was given 10 $\frac{4}{5}$ boxes of white board markers. She was later given 3 $\frac{6}{8}$ more boxes of white board markers. How many markers did she receive altogether?

❑ Circle key words & relevant information.

Operation: _____

Information: _____

_____

Number Sentence: _____

Solution Sentence: _____

_____

work space

**13.** There were 9 $\frac{5}{6}$ crates of watermelons left at the market. A farmer brought in 18 more crates of watermelons. How many crates of watermelons were there in total?

❑ Circle key words & relevant information.

Operation: _____

Information: _____

_____

Number Sentence: _____

Solution Sentence: _____

_____

work space

**14.** A baby kangaroo was born $\frac{3}{4}$ of a month early. At birth her weight was 4 $\frac{1}{2}$ lbs which is $\frac{9}{10}$ smaller than the average size of a newborn kangaroo. How much does an average newborn kangaroo weigh?

❑ Circle key words & relevant information.

Operation: _____

Information: _____

_____

Number Sentence: _____

Solution Sentence: _____

_____

work space

**15.** Brian bought 18 $\frac{4}{5}$ pounds of dog food for his pet. When he got home he realized he already had 5 $\frac{3}{8}$ pounds of dog food. How much dog food did he have in total?

❑ Circle key words & relevant information.

Operation: _____

Information: _____

_____

Number Sentence: _____

Solution Sentence: _____

_____

> work space

**16.** Visiting hours at a hospital happen twice per day. In the morning the hospital is open for visitors for $\frac{5}{6}$ of an hour and in the afternoon it is open for $\frac{7}{9}$ of an hour. How long is the hospital open for visitors daily?

❑ Circle key words & relevant information.

Operation: _____

Information: _____

_____

Number Sentence: _____

Solution Sentence: _____

_____

> work space

10

**17.** Kate used $\frac{2}{5}$ cups of flour for a cake and later used $\frac{6}{8}$ cups of flour to bake cookies. How much flour did she use in total?

☐ Circle key words & relevant information.

Operation: _____

Information: _____

_____

Number Sentence: _____

Solution Sentence: _____

_____

work space

**18.** Zach traveled $\frac{7}{10}$ hours from his apartment to his office. After work, he traveled $\frac{2}{4}$ hours to a restaurant to meet a friend. He then traveled $\frac{5}{8}$ hours back home. How much did Zach travel that day?

☐ Circle key words & relevant information.

Operation: _____

Information: _____

_____

Number Sentence: _____

Solution Sentence: _____

_____

work space

11

**19.** Frankie completed $^6/_7$ of his nightly homework on Monday. He then completed $^2/_3$ of his nightly homework on Tuesday and $^7/_9$ of his nightly homework on Wednesday. How much of his homework did he complete?

❑ Circle key words & relevant information.

Operation: _____

Information: _____

_____

Number Sentence: _____

Solution Sentence: _____

_____

> work space

**20.** Nicole wanted to buy new equipment to practice playing sports. She went to the store for 2 hours and spent $^1/_3$ of her money on shorts and another $^3/_6$ of her money on a basketball. She used another $^1/_{12}$ of her money to buy badminton rackets for her 2 siblings. What fraction of her money did she spend on sports equipment in all?

❑ Circle key words & relevant information.

Operation: _____

Information: _____

_____

Number Sentence: _____

Solution Sentence: _____

_____

> work space

# COINS 4 – Section 2
## Using COINS to Solve Fraction Word Problems
## Subtracting Fractions

When you read a word problem, certain key words can help you determine how to correctly solve the problem.

**Fraction word problems**
*Remember the following words:*

### Subtraction

- take away
- left
- fewer
- how many more
- difference

When you solve word problems using **COINS**, remember to read the problem, then solve it as follows:

**C**ircle: Circle the key words and relevant information (and cross out any irrelevant information).

**O**peration: : **X**, **÷**, etc.

**I**nformation: Write the relevant information.

**N**umber Sentence: Write the math problem.

**S**olution Sentence: Write the solution as a full sentence.

# Complete the Problems

Use **COINS** to solve these fraction word problems. Remember to circle the key words, draw pictures if necessary, and cross out any extra information. Then complete the steps using the **COINS Strategy**.

**1.** Gabriel planted a tree on his birthday. In 2018 it stood 3 $\frac{4}{5}$ feet tall and in 2019 it stood at 9 $\frac{5}{6}$ feet tall. How many feet did the tree grow in a year?

❑ Circle key words & relevant information.

Operation: _____

Information: _____

_____

Number Sentence: _____

Solution Sentence: _____

_____

work space

**2.** Candance made 7 cakes and gave away 2 $\frac{1}{2}$ cakes. How much cake was left over?

❑ Circle key words & relevant information.

Operation: _____

Information: _____

_____

Number Sentence: _____

Solution Sentence: _____

_____

work space

**3.** Kevin had 67 $\frac{4}{5}$ yards of twine.
If he used 45 $\frac{2}{7}$ yards for crocheting,
how much twine did he have left?

❑ Circle key words & relevant information.

Operation: _____

Information: _____

_____

Number Sentence: _____

Solution Sentence: _____

_____

work space

**4.** Valerie puts $\frac{5}{7}$ of a cup of peanut butter
and $\frac{6}{18}$ of a cup of jelly on her sandwich.
How much more peanut butter does
Valerie have on her sandwich than jelly?

❑ Circle key words & relevant information.

Operation: _____

Information: _____

_____

Number Sentence: _____

Solution Sentence: _____

_____

work space

**5.** Celia made an apple pie. She used $\frac{2}{3}$ of a tablespoon of cinnam on and $\frac{5}{7}$ of a tablespoon of nutmeg. How much more nutmeg than cinnamon did Celia use?

❑ Circle key words & relevant information.

Operation: _____

Information: _____

_____

Number Sentence: _____

Solution Sentence: _____

_____

work space

**6.** Susan finished her math assignment 3 $\frac{1}{2}$ in hours and Natalie finished the same assignment in 5 $\frac{4}{5}$ hours. How much longer did Natalie take to do the same assignment?

❑ Circle key words & relevant information.

Operation: _____

Information: _____

_____

Number Sentence: _____

Solution Sentence: _____

_____

work space

**7.** Shane had 55 $\frac{1}{9}$ pounds of candy. He gave out 33 $\frac{4}{5}$ pounds over the span of a few weeks. How much candy did he have left?

❑ Circle key words & relevant information.

Operation: _____

Information: _____

_____

Number Sentence: _____

Solution Sentence: _____

_____

work space

**8.** Conor answered $\frac{5}{7}$ of the total number of questions on his history test. If $\frac{2}{3}$ of his answers were correct, what fraction of questions did he answer incorrectly?

❑ Circle key words & relevant information.

Operation: _____

Information: _____

_____

Number Sentence: _____

Solution Sentence: _____

_____

work space

**9.** Vicky bought $\frac{26}{4}$ pounds of chicken but the recipe called for 8 pounds of chicken. Did she have enough? If not, how many more pounds of chicken did she need?

❏ Circle key words & relevant information.

Operation: _____

Information: _____

_____

Number Sentence: _____

Solution Sentence: _____

_____

| work space |
|---|

**10.** A bottle of orange juice can hold $\frac{8}{9}$ of a cup of liquid. If Erin pours $\frac{2}{3}$ cup of orange juice into a bottle, how much space is left in the bottle?

❏ Circle key words & relevant information.

Operation: _____

Information: _____

_____

Number Sentence: _____

Solution Sentence: _____

_____

| work space |
|---|

**11.** In a school auditorium, ⅕ of the students performed on stage, ⅞ of the students were in the stage crew, and the rest were sitting and enjoying the performance. What fraction of the students were in the audience?

❏ Circle key words & relevant information.

Operation: _____

Information: _____

_____

Number Sentence: _____

Solution Sentence: _____

_____

work space

**12.** The Fitzgerald family went apple picking. The youngest sibling had 4 ⁵⁄₇ pounds of apples at the end of the day and the oldest sibling had ³⁶⁄₇ pounds of apples. Which sibling picked more apples and how do you know?

❏ Circle key words & relevant information.

Operation: _____

Information: _____

_____

Number Sentence: _____

Solution Sentence: _____

_____

work space

**13.** When Peter began his road trip, his gas tank was $\frac{8}{9}$ full of fuel. At the end of his trip, he had $\frac{1}{7}$ gallons of fuel left in his tank. How much gas did his car use?

❑ Circle key words & relevant information.

Operation: _____

Information: _____

_____

Number Sentence: _____

Solution Sentence: _____

_____

work space

**14.** A skyscraper being built in NYC was 20 $\frac{3}{4}$ feet tall in January. In May it was 140 $\frac{5}{9}$ tall. If the building was set to be 330 $\frac{4}{6}$ feet tall, how many more feet needed to be built?

❑ Circle key words & relevant information.

Operation: _____

Information: _____

_____

Number Sentence: _____

Solution Sentence: _____

_____

work space

20

**15.** Two kinds of fish can be found in a small tank that is 6 $\frac{4}{7}$ feet long. The yellow fish is 3 $\frac{2}{15}$ feet long and the orange fish is $\frac{3}{9}$ feet long. How much shorter is the orange fish than the yellow fish?

❏ Circle key words & relevant information.

Operation: _____

Information: _____

_____

Number Sentence: _____

Solution Sentence: _____

_____

work space

**16.** Sally reads $\frac{4}{15}$ of her book on Thursday and $\frac{2}{6}$ of her book over the weekend. How much more does she need to read until she finishes the book?

❏ Circle key words & relevant information.

Operation: _____

Information: _____

_____

Number Sentence: _____

Solution Sentence: _____

_____

work space

**17.** Allison walked 3 $\frac{4}{5}$ blocks and jogged 6 $\frac{4}{15}$ blocks. How many more blocks did she jog rather than walk?

☐ Circle key words & relevant information.

Operation: _____

Information: _____

_____

Number Sentence: _____

Solution Sentence: _____

_____

work space

**18.** A farmer sold $\frac{1}{2}$ of his sheep one day and $\frac{3}{8}$ of them the next day. What fraction of his sheep did he have left?

☐ Circle key words & relevant information.

Operation: _____

Information: _____

_____

Number Sentence: _____

Solution Sentence: _____

_____

work space

**19.** Sarah's closet is 9 feet tall and her sister's closet is $19\frac{3}{4}$ feet tall. What is the difference in the heights of the closets?

☐ Circle key words & relevant information.

Operation: _____

Information: _____

_____

Number Sentence: _____

Solution Sentence: _____

_____

work space

**20.** A baseball team had $\frac{1}{18}$ of its team out for injuries. $\frac{3}{8}$ of the team were on the bench and the rest were on the field. What fraction of the team was playing on the field?

☐ Circle key words & relevant information.

Operation: _____

Information: _____

_____

Number Sentence: _____

Solution Sentence: _____

_____

work space

# COINS 4 – Section 3
## Using COINS to Solve Fraction Word Problems
## Adding & Subtracting Fractions

When you read a word problem, certain key words can help you determine how to correctly solve the problem.

**Fraction word problems: Do I add or subtract?**

*Remember the following key words:*

| **Addition** | **Substraction** |
|---|---|
| • add | • take away |
| • altogether | • left |
| • in all | • fewer |
| • sum | • how many more |
| • combined | • difference |
| • in total | |

When you solve word problems using **COINS**, remember to read the problem, then solve it as follows:

**C**ircle: <u>Circle the key words and relevant information (and cross out any irrelevant information).</u>

**O**peration: : <u>**X**</u>, <u>**÷**</u>, etc.

**I**nformation: <u>Write the relevant information</u>.

**N**umber Sentence: <u>Write the math problem</u>.

**S**olution Sentence: <u>Write the solution as a full sentence</u>.

24

# Complete the Problems

Use the **COINS** to solve these fraction word problems. Remember to circle the key words, draw pictures if necessary, and cross out any extra information. Then complete the steps in **COINS Strategy**.

**1.** Jordan grated ⅚ of a block of cheese to make a pasta dish. What fraction of the block was left?

❑ Circle key words & relevant information.

Operation: _____

Information: _____

_____

Number Sentence: _____

Solution Sentence: _____

_____

work space

**2.** A store owner had 13 ⅘ boxes of candles. She received a shipment of 7 ⅚ boxes of candles the next day. How many boxes of candles did she have altogether?

❑ Circle key words & relevant information.

Operation: _____

Information: _____

_____

Number Sentence: _____

Solution Sentence: _____

_____

work space

**3.** A farmer had 11 ¼ sacks of corn. He then added 3 ⅘ sacks of corn. How many corn sacks did he have altogether?

❑ Circle key words & relevant information.

Operation: _____

Information: _____

_____

Number Sentence: _____

Solution Sentence: _____

_____

work space

**4.** Paige is mixing fruit salad. She combines 4 ½ cups of strawberries, 6 ¾ cups of pineapple and cups of kiwi. How much fruit did she include altogether?

❑ Circle key words & relevant information.

Operation: _____

Information: _____

_____

Number Sentence: _____

Solution Sentence: _____

_____

work space

**5.** Jack decided to paint his house. He needed 5 $\frac{4}{6}$ gallons of blue paint, 6 $\frac{7}{8}$ gallons of white paint, and 3 $\frac{7}{8}$ gallons of maroon paint. How many gallons of paint did Jack need altogether?

❏ Circle key words & relevant information.

Operation: _____

Information: _____

_____

Number Sentence: _____

Solution Sentence: _____

_____

work space

**6.** Rachel's shoe size was 3 $\frac{1}{2}$ when she was in 1st grade. Now her shoe size is 9. How many sizes did her feet grow?

❏ Circle key words & relevant information.

Operation: _____

Information: _____

_____

Number Sentence: _____

Solution Sentence: _____

_____

work space

**7.** Sarah is making jugs of drinks for a party. If she adds 16 $\frac{4}{5}$ cups of lemonade and 18 $\frac{2}{3}$ cups of iced tea, how much liquid will she have in her jug?

❏ Circle key words & relevant information.

Operation: _____

Information: _____

_____

Number Sentence: _____

Solution Sentence: _____

_____

work space

**8.** Henry earned $320.50. He purchased a video game for $98.25. How much money did he have left after the purchase?

❏ Circle key words & relevant information.

Operation: _____

Information: _____

_____

Number Sentence: _____

Solution Sentence: _____

_____

work space

**9.** Ethan's walk to the store usually take 18 minutes. Today it took him $57/2$ minutes to walk to the store. How much longer did it take him to walk today?

❑ Circle key words & relevant information.

Operation: _____

Information: _____

_____

Number Sentence: _____

Solution Sentence: _____

_____

> work space

**10.** A pencil is 6 inches long. A special birthday pencil is $6/4$ inches longer than a regular pencil. How long is a special birthday pencil?

❑ Circle key words & relevant information.

Operation: _____

Information: _____

_____

Number Sentence: _____

Solution Sentence: _____

_____

> work space

**11.** Tasha drove 6 $\frac{4}{5}$ hours to her cousin's house. When she drove back she covered the same distance in $2\frac{1}{6}$ hours. How much less time was the return trip?

❑ Circle key words & relevant information.

Operation: _____

Information: _____

_____

Number Sentence: _____

Solution Sentence: _____

_____

work space

**12.** Noah spent 5 hours baking cookies and pies for a bake sale. If it took him 2 $\frac{3}{4}$ hours to bake the cookies, how long did it take him to bake the pies?

❑ Circle key words & relevant information.

Operation: _____

Information: _____

_____

Number Sentence: _____

Solution Sentence: _____

_____

work space

**13.** Gabby had 7 ⅔ boxes of cereal in her kitchen. She went through 9½ boxes in 3 months. How many cereal boxes remained?

☐ Circle key words & relevant information.

Operation: _____

Information: _____

_____

Number Sentence: _____

Solution Sentence: _____

_____

work space

**14.** Olivia drove to a party 7 ⁵⁄₇ miles away from her home. If she stopped to pick up a cake 3 miles away from the party, how far did she already travel?

☐ Circle key words & relevant information.

Operation: _____

Information: _____

_____

Number Sentence: _____

Solution Sentence: _____

_____

work space

**15.** Daniel practiced the violin for 43 $\frac{2}{9}$ minutes over the weekend. He practiced for 105 $\frac{3}{4}$ minutes during the school week. How many minutes did Daniel practice the violin for altogether?

❑ Circle key words & relevant information.

Operation: _____

Information: _____

_____

Number Sentence: _____

Solution Sentence: _____

_____

work space

**16.** Cassie has 11 $\frac{4}{6}$ jars of peanut butter and $\frac{7}{2}$ jars of jelly. How many more jars of peanut butter does she have than jelly?

❑ Circle key words & relevant information.

Operation: _____

Information: _____

_____

Number Sentence: _____

Solution Sentence: _____

_____

work space

**17.** Avery recycles 6 $\frac{5}{6}$ pounds of goods each month. How many pounds of recycled goods will she have recycled after 3 months?

❑ Circle key words & relevant information.

Operation: _____

Information: _____

_____

Number Sentence: _____

Solution Sentence: _____

_____

work space

**18.** A recipe for salad dressing calls for 3 tablespoons of lemon juice, 4 $\frac{3}{5}$ tablespoons of olive oil, and 6 $\frac{2}{7}$ tablespoons of balsamic vinegar. How many tablespoons of liquid are needed altogether?

❑ Circle key words & relevant information.

Operation: _____

Information: _____

_____

Number Sentence: _____

Solution Sentence: _____

_____

work space

**19.** Charlotte practiced basketball for 3 hours on Monday and 6 ⅗ hours on Tuesday. If she practiced for 10 hours in total by Wednesday, how many hours did she practice on Wednesday?

❑ Circle key words & relevant information.

Operation: _____

Information: _____

_____

Number Sentence: _____

Solution Sentence: _____

_____

work space

**20.** Ava is cleaning the windows in her home. If she cleans 5 ⅔ square feet of windows on the first two days and cleans 7 ⅜ square feet of windows on the third day, how many square feet of windows did she clean in three days?

❑ Circle key words & relevant information.

Operation: _____

Information: _____

_____

Number Sentence: _____

Solution Sentence: _____

_____

work space

# COINS 4 – Section 4
## Using COINS to Solve Advanced Fraction Word Problems
## Multiplying Fractions

When you read a word problem, certain <u>questions</u> can help you determine how to correctly solve the problem.

**Fraction word problems: Multiplication**

- Is the problem asking for a total?

- Are you taking part of the total?

- Are you taking part of the part?

- Are you trying to determine a certain amount you need for something?

When you solve word problems using **COINS**, remember to read the problem, then solve it as follows:

**C**ircle: <u>Circle the key words and relevant information (and cross out any irrelevant information).</u>

**O**peration: : <u>**X**</u>, <u>**÷**</u>, etc.

**I**nformation: <u>Write the relevant information</u>.

**N**umber Sentence: <u>Write the math problem</u>.

**S**olution Sentence: <u>Write the solution as a full sentence</u>.

# Complete the Problems

Use the **COINS Strategy** to solve these advanced fraction word problems. Remember to circle the key words, draw pictures if necessary, and cross out any extra information. Then complete the steps in **COINS Strategy**.

**1.** Jacob read ⅜ of a book every day for 15 days. How many books did he read altogether?

❑ Circle key words & relevant information.

Operation: _____

Information: _____

_____

Number Sentence: _____

Solution Sentence: _____

_____

work space

**2.** Adrienne used 7 ⅕ teaspoon of salt for her cake recipe. If she made 11 cakes, how much salt did she use?

❑ Circle key words & relevant information.

Operation: _____

Information: _____

_____

Number Sentence: _____

Solution Sentence: _____

_____

work space

**3.** Kelly is playing a video game where each round lasts $\frac{7}{12}$ of an hour. She plans to play 16 rounds. How much time will it take in total?

❏ Circle key words & relevant information.

Operation: _____

Information: _____

_____

Number Sentence: _____

Solution Sentence: _____

_____

work space

**4.** Carlos wants to put $\frac{3}{8}$ of a cup of bird seed in each of the bird cages in his pet shop. He has 14 bird cages. How much bird seed will he need altogether?

❏ Circle key words & relevant information.

Operation: _____

Information: _____

_____

Number Sentence: _____

Solution Sentence: _____

_____

work space

**5.** Sharon grew tomatoes this summer and used them to make 16 bowls of tomato sauce. Each bowl contained $\frac{4}{5}$ of a gallon of sauce. How much tomato sauce did she make altogether?

❑ Circle key words & relevant information.

Operation: _____

Information: _____

_____

Number Sentence: _____

Solution Sentence: _____

_____

work space

**6.** Mary is picking songs to play during a slideshow. The songs are each 3 $\frac{1}{2}$ minutes long and there are 16 songs in the slideshow. How long will the slideshow be?

❑ Circle key words & relevant information.

Operation: _____

Information: _____

_____

Number Sentence: _____

Solution Sentence: _____

_____

work space

**7.** According to a recipe, each batch of pancake mix can make 12 pancakes. Margaret is making 3 batches for a brunch party. If each batch needs 3 $\frac{2}{15}$ cups of milk, how much milk does she need in total?

❑ Circle key words & relevant information.

Operation: _____

Information: _____

_____

Number Sentence: _____

Solution Sentence: _____

_____

work space

**8.** A stretch of road needs repairs. Workers can repair 2 $\frac{1}{4}$ mile of road per week. If the project takes 16 weeks, how many miles of road will they repair?

❑ Circle key words & relevant information.

Operation: _____

Information: _____

_____

Number Sentence: _____

Solution Sentence: _____

_____

work space

**9.** Matt has ⅘ of a tank of fuel in his car. He uses ¹⁄₁₀ of a tank per day. How many days will his fuel last?

❑ Circle key words & relevant information.

Operation: _____

Information: _____

_____

Number Sentence: _____

Solution Sentence: _____

_____

work space

**10.** A pizza is cut into slices that are each ⅙ of the whole. Paul is going to eat ½ of the whole pizza. How many slices will his friend John eat?

❑ Circle key words & relevant information.

Operation: _____

Information: _____

_____

Number Sentence: _____

Solution Sentence: _____

_____

work space

**11.** Liz finish a 200-meter race in $\frac{5}{12}$ of a minute. The winner finished the race in $\frac{21}{25}$ of Liz's time. How much time did the winner take to finish the race?

❑ Circle key words & relevant information.

Operation: _____

Information: _____

Number Sentence: _____

Solution Sentence: _____

work space

**12.** A pizza restaurant used its final batch of pizza sauce to make some pizzas. The chef put $\frac{1}{6}$ of a cup of sauce on each pizza and made 22 pizzas. How much sauce did the chef use?

❑ Circle key words & relevant information.

Operation: _____

Information: _____

Number Sentence: _____

Solution Sentence: _____

work space

**13.** Lucas is competing in a triathlon against his brother. If Lucas finishes the race in 2 ⅗ hours and his brother finishes the race in twice the amount of time as Lucas, how much time does it take for Lucas' brother to finish the race?

☐ Circle key words & relevant information.

Operation: _____

Information: _____

_____

Number Sentence: _____

Solution Sentence: _____

_____

work space

**14.** There are 24 hours in a day and Willie sleeps for ⅜ of it. How many hours does Willie sleep?

☐ Circle key words & relevant information.

Operation: _____

Information: _____

_____

Number Sentence: _____

Solution Sentence: _____

_____

work space

**15.** Alex is using her phone. The phone's battery life is down to ⅖ and it drains ⅑ of its life every hour. How many hours will her battery last?

☐ Circle key words & relevant information.

Operation: _____

Information: _____

_____

Number Sentence: _____

Solution Sentence: _____

_____

work space

**16.** Anna usually rides her bike about 1 ⅕ hours every day. The distance between the library and school is ⅞ mile. Yesterday her bike had a problem and Anna only rode her bike ⅔ of the way from school to the library and walked the rest of the way. How far did she ride her bike?

☐ Circle key words & relevant information.

Operation: _____

Information: _____

_____

Number Sentence: _____

Solution Sentence: _____

_____

work space

**17.** Pam took out 8 glasses and poured juice from a pitcher. The capacity of each glass was $\frac{3}{10}$ cups. If there was enough juice for 6 glasses, how much juice was there?

❑ Circle key words & relevant information.

Operation: _____

Information: _____

_____

Number Sentence: _____

Solution Sentence: _____

_____

work space

**18.** According to a recipe, $\frac{9}{20}$ ounces of sugar is needed to make 6 cookies. Ashley decided to use only a third of the sugar to make it healthier. How much sugar did Ashley use?

❑ Circle key words & relevant information.

Operation: _____

Information: _____

_____

Number Sentence: _____

Solution Sentence: _____

_____

work space

**19.** The height of the ceiling in a nursery is $^{35}/_8$ feet high and the height of the ceiling in the master bedroom is $^{23}/_5$ times as high as the ceiling in the nursery. How high is the ceiling in the master bedroom?

❏ Circle key words & relevant information.

Operation: _____

Information: _____

_____

Number Sentence: _____

Solution Sentence: _____

_____

work space

**20.** Grant feeds each of his dogs $^1/_{10}$ of a can of food each day. He uses a total of $^3/_5$ of a can of food each day. How many dogs does Grant have?

❏ Circle key words & relevant information.

Operation: _____

Information: _____

_____

Number Sentence: _____

Solution Sentence: _____

_____

work space

# COINS 4 – Section 5
## Using COINS to Solve Advanced Fraction Word Problems
## Dividing Fractions

When you read a word problem, certain <u>questions</u> can help you determine how to correctly solve the problem.

**Fraction word problems: Division**

- Are you dividing a given amount into equal groups?

- Are you taking an amount and sorting it, breaking it up or cutting it into equal groups?

- Are you using an equal amount of a total and looking for how much used?

When you solve word problems using **COINS**, remember to read the problem, then solve it as follows:

**C**ircle: <u>Circle the key words and relevant information (and cross out any irrelevant information)</u>.

**O**peration: : <u>**X**</u>, <u>**÷**</u>, etc.

**I**nformation: <u>Write the relevant information</u>.

**N**umber Sentence: <u>Write the math problem</u>.

**S**olution Sentence: <u>Write the solution as a full sentence</u>.

# Complete the Problems

Use the **COINS Strategy** to solve these advanced fraction word problems. Remember to circle the key words, draw pictures if necessary, and cross out any extra information. Then complete the steps in **COINS Strategy**.

**1.** Annie uses $\frac{10}{4}$ cup of sugar to make 10 brownies. How much sugar is needed to make 1 brownie?

❑ Circle key words & relevant information.

Operation: _____

Information: _____

_____

Number Sentence: _____

Solution Sentence: _____

_____

> work space

**2.** Martin wrapped 24 gifts using $\frac{45}{3}$ rolls of wrapping paper. If each gift was the same size, how much wrapping paper did each gift require?

❑ Circle key words & relevant information.

Operation: _____

Information: _____

_____

Number Sentence: _____

Solution Sentence: _____

_____

> work space

**3.** A swimming pool is open for 8 ½ hours during a day. If there is one lifeguard on duty at a time and shifts are 1 ½ hours long, how many lifeguards are needed per day?

❑ Circle key words & relevant information.

Operation: _____

Information: _____

_____

Number Sentence: _____

Solution Sentence: _____

_____

work space

**4.** Alex and his sister decided to clean $\frac{8}{9}$ of the total area of their house. If they split the chore equally, what fraction of the total area did each of them clean?

❑ Circle key words & relevant information.

Operation: _____

Information: _____

_____

Number Sentence: _____

Solution Sentence: _____

_____

work space

**5.** Rebecca eats ⅔ cups of granola for breakfast every day. If the bag of granola contains a total of 30 cups, how many days will it take her to finish the entire bag of granola?

❑ Circle key words & relevant information.

Operation: _____

Information: _____

_____

Number Sentence: _____

Solution Sentence: _____

_____

work space

**6.** Zach collects dominoes and he keeps them in small boxes of equal amounts in his room. If he keeps $^{54}\!/_4$ pounds of dominoes in 6 boxes, how many dominoes are in each box?

❑ Circle key words & relevant information.

Operation: _____

Information: _____

_____

Number Sentence: _____

Solution Sentence: _____

_____

work space

**7.** Katie is a cyclist who covers $\frac{18}{2}$ miles in a series of 18 laps. How many miles make up one lap?

❏ Circle key words & relevant information.

Operation: _____

Information: _____

_____

Number Sentence: _____

Solution Sentence: _____

_____

| work space |
| --- |
| |

**8.** A small restaurant made $\frac{48}{2}$ cups of soup for the lunch shift. If each bowl held 4 cups of soup and there was no soup leftover, how many bowls of soup were sold?

❏ Circle key words & relevant information.

Operation: _____

Information: _____

_____

Number Sentence: _____

Solution Sentence: _____

_____

| work space |
| --- |
| |

**9.** A total of $\frac{120}{4}$ pounds of seaweed washed up on a beach. If cleaners put an equal amount of the seaweed into 5 buckets, how many pounds of seaweed went into each bucket?

❏ Circle key words & relevant information.

Operation: _____

Information: _____

_____

Number Sentence: _____

Solution Sentence: _____

_____

work space

**10.** Avery made $\frac{66}{3}$ gallons of lemonade to share equally between her 9 friends. How much lemonade did each friend receive?

❏ Circle key words & relevant information.

Operation: _____

Information: _____

_____

Number Sentence: _____

Solution Sentence: _____

_____

work space

51

**11.** Olivia was able to fill 4 $\frac{2}{5}$ equal sized boxes with jars of jelly. If she packaged 33 jars of jelly, how many boxes did she use?

☐ Circle key words & relevant information.

Operation: _____

Information: _____

_____

Number Sentence: _____

Solution Sentence: _____

_____

work space

**12.** A 10 inch Italian hero sandwich was ordered for a party. If each section cut was $\frac{2}{5}$ inches long, how many sections of the sandwich were there?

☐ Circle key words & relevant information.

Operation: _____

Information: _____

_____

Number Sentence: _____

Solution Sentence: _____

_____

work space

**13.** A mother gave out pizza at her child's birthday party. If she gave each child ³⁄14 of a slice of pizza and she gave out 18 slices, how many children received pizza?

❏ Circle key words & relevant information.

Operation: _____

Information: _____

_____

Number Sentence: _____

Solution Sentence: _____

_____

work space

**14.** A turtle moved ¼ of a mile every hour. If the turtle traveled 16 miles, how many hours did it take?

❏ Circle key words & relevant information.

Operation: _____

Information: _____

_____

Number Sentence: _____

Solution Sentence: _____

_____

work space

**15.** Benny needs 5 $\frac{6}{11}$ of flour to make a pie. If Benny has 33 cups of flour, how many pies can he make?

☐ Circle key words & relevant information.

Operation: _____

Information: _____

_____

Number Sentence: _____

Solution Sentence: _____

_____

work space

**16.** Paul is planting rows of tomatoes in his backyard. If he has 24 square feet in his yard and each row of tomatoes needs 4 $\frac{1}{3}$ square feet, how many rows of tomatoes can he plant?

☐ Circle key words & relevant information.

Operation: _____

Information: _____

_____

Number Sentence: _____

Solution Sentence: _____

_____

work space

**17.** Amy is going to make 17 pints of hot chocolate for her classmates. If each mug holds $^{26}\!/_3$ pints of liquid, how many mugs can she fill?

❑ Circle key words & relevant information.

Operation: _____

Information: _____

_____

Number Sentence: _____

Solution Sentence: _____

_____

work space

**18.** Lisa and some friends bought 6 pounds of chocolate at the store. If each friend wants $\frac{1}{2}$ pound of chocolate, how many friends can share the chocolate?

❑ Circle key words & relevant information.

Operation: _____

Information: _____

_____

Number Sentence: _____

Solution Sentence: _____

_____

work space

**19.** A track coach wants her athletes to run 6 miles around a track. If each lap is $^{17}/_8$ of a mile, how many laps will each runner need to complete?

☐ Circle key words & relevant information.

Operation: _____

Information: _____

_____

Number Sentence: _____

Solution Sentence: _____

_____

work space

**20.** Brad made brownies for his classmates. He made enough brownies so that each student could have more than one. If Brad made 23 $^1/_4$ brownies and there were 18 students in the class, how many brownies did each child receive?

☐ Circle key words & relevant information.

Operation: _____

Information: _____

_____

Number Sentence: _____

Solution Sentence: _____

_____

work space

# COINS 4 – Section 6
## Using COINS to Solve Advanced Fraction Word Problems
## Multiplying & Dividing Fractions

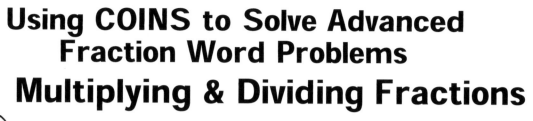

When you read a word problem, certain <u>questions</u> can help you determine how to correctly solve the problem.

**Fraction word problems: Do I multiply or divide?**

### Multiplication

- Is the problem asking for a total?
- Are you taking part of the total?
- Are you taking part of the part?
- Are you trying to determine a certain amount you need for something?

### Division

- Are you dividing a given amount into equal groups?
- Are you taking an amount and sorting it, breaking it up or cutting it into equal groups?
- Are you using an equal amount of a total and looking for how much used?

When you solve word problems using **COINS**, remember to read the problem, then solve it as follows:

**C**ircle: <u>Circle the key words and relevant information (and cross out any irrelevant information).</u>

**O**peration: : <u>**X**</u>, <u>÷</u>, etc.

**I**nformation: <u>Write the relevant information</u>.

**N**umber Sentence: <u>Write the math problem</u>.

**S**olution Sentence: <u>Write the solution as a full sentence</u>.

# Complete the Problems

Use the **COINS Strategy** to solve these advanced fraction word problems. Remember to circle the key words, draw pictures if necessary, and cross out any extra information. Then complete the steps in **COINS Strategy**.

**1.** Beth exercises by cycling and running. She cycles for 3 $\frac{1}{5}$ miles and then runs $\frac{3}{4}$ of the distance she cycles. How many miles does she run?

☐ Circle key words & relevant information.

Operation: _____

Information: _____

_____

Number Sentence: _____

Solution Sentence: _____

_____

work space

**2.** Pat drives $\frac{10}{4}$ miles a day. How many days will it take Pat to cover a distance of 18 $\frac{1}{4}$ miles?

☐ Circle key words & relevant information.

Operation: _____

Information: _____

_____

Number Sentence: _____

Solution Sentence: _____

_____

work space

**3.** Jill and Simon are picking cranberries. Jill picks 11 $\frac{2}{3}$ ounces and Simon picks $\frac{7}{5}$ times more cranberries than Jill picks. How many ounces of cranberries does Simon pick?

❑ Circle key words & relevant information.

Operation: _____

Information: _____

_____

Number Sentence: _____

Solution Sentence: _____

_____

work space

**4.** Aaron prepares 5 $\frac{3}{7}$ pounds of turkey to serve at his Thanksgiving dinner. If there's $\frac{4}{6}$ of a pound of turkey in one serving, how many servings are there?

❑ Circle key words & relevant information.

Operation: _____

Information: _____

_____

Number Sentence: _____

Solution Sentence: _____

_____

work space

**5.** Kelly went to a carnival and rode the carousel 3 times. If each ride lasted 9 ⅗ minutes, how many minutes did Kelly ride in all?

☐ Circle key words & relevant information.

Operation: _____

Information: _____

_____

Number Sentence: _____

Solution Sentence: _____

_____

> work space

**6.** Allie ate ⁴⁄₃ plates of pancakes. Ryan ate ⁹⁄₄ times as many pancakes as Allie did. How many pancakes did Ryan eat?

☐ Circle key words & relevant information.

Operation: _____

Information: _____

_____

Number Sentence: _____

Solution Sentence: _____

_____

> work space

**7.** Jade has been typing notes at a consistent speed. If she types 16 ½ pages in ⁷⁄₃ hours, how many pages does she type in one hour?

❑ Circle key words & relevant information.

Operation: _____

Information: _____

_____

Number Sentence: _____

Solution Sentence: _____

_____

work space

**8.** Jackie has 3 ³⁄₅ gallons of milk in her refrigerater and she drinks ²⁄₃ of it. How much milk does Jackie drink?

❑ Circle key words & relevant information.

Operation: _____

Information: _____

_____

Number Sentence: _____

Solution Sentence: _____

_____

work space

**9.** A water hose fills $\frac{1}{6}$ of a bucket in two minutes. How many minutes will it take to fill 2 $\frac{1}{8}$ buckets?

❑ Circle key words & relevant information.

Operation: _____

Information: _____

_____

Number Sentence: _____

Solution Sentence: _____

_____

> work space

**10.** Jimmy drank $\frac{3}{4}$ of a carton of orange juice. If he drank 4 $\frac{8}{9}$ times as much apple juice as he did orange juice, how many cartons of apple juice did he drink?

❑ Circle key words & relevant information.

Operation: _____

Information: _____

_____

Number Sentence: _____

Solution Sentence: _____

_____

> work space

**11.** Julie finished a five mile race in 42 $^{12}/_{15}$ minutes. The winner of the race finished it in $^2/_5$ of the time Julie did. How many minutes did the winner take to finish the race?

❑ Circle key words & relevant information.

Operation: _____

Information: _____

_____

Number Sentence: _____

Solution Sentence: _____

_____

work space

**12.** Ava makes sofa covers. If one cover requires 16 $^2/_5$ yards of fabric, how many covers can she make with 33 $^{15}/_8$ yards of fabric?

❑ Circle key words & relevant information.

Operation: _____

Information: _____

_____

Number Sentence: _____

Solution Sentence: _____

_____

work space

**13.** Craig requires 19 $\frac{2}{7}$ ounces of flour to make a batch cookies. How many ounces will he require to make $\frac{7}{3}$ batches?

❑ Circle key words & relevant information.

Operation: _____

Information: _____

_____

Number Sentence: _____

Solution Sentence: _____

_____

work space

**14.** Peter walked $\frac{13}{2}$ miles in $\frac{3}{2}$ hours. How many miles did he walk in an hour?

❑ Circle key words & relevant information.

Operation: _____

Information: _____

_____

Number Sentence: _____

Solution Sentence: _____

_____

work space

**15.** If it requires $\frac{1}{15}$ of a pound of ground turkey to make a meatball, how many meatballs can be made with $\frac{10}{9}$ pounds of ground turkey?

❑ Circle key words & relevant information.

Operation: _____

Information: _____

_____

Number Sentence: _____

Solution Sentence: _____

_____

work space

**16.** Jenny distrbutes 23 $\frac{1}{3}$ cups of compost between her pots so that each pot 1 $\frac{2}{3}$ receives cups of compost. How many pots are there?

❑ Circle key words & relevant information.

Operation: _____

Information: _____

_____

Number Sentence: _____

Solution Sentence: _____

_____

work space

**17.** A mini slide at a fun fair is 4 ⅜ feet high. There's a larger slide that's 5 ⅖ times as high as the mini slide. What is the height of the larger slide?

❑ Circle key words & relevant information.

Operation: _____

Information: _____

_____

Number Sentence: _____

Solution Sentence: _____

_____

work space

**18.** At the school dance, slow songs were played that lasted a total of 15 ¾ minutes. If each song was exactly 1 ¾ minutes, how many slow songs were there?

❑ Circle key words & relevant information.

Operation: _____

Information: _____

_____

Number Sentence: _____

Solution Sentence: _____

_____

work space

**19.** Rachel has a tub that holds 52 ⅙ gallons of water. Her sister has a larger tub that holds ⁹⁄₃ times as much water as Rachel's tub. How much water does her sister's tub hold?

❏ Circle key words & relevant information.

Operation: _____

Information: _____

_____

Number Sentence: _____

Solution Sentence: _____

_____

work space

**20.** Mike needs 5 ½ cups of pasta to make a dish. If he has 26 ⅔ cups of pasta, how many dishes can he make?

❏ Circle key words & relevant information.

Operation: _____

Information: _____

_____

Number Sentence: _____

Solution Sentence: _____

_____

work space

# COINS 4 – Section 7
## Using COINS to Solve Word Problems
# Multiplying & Dividing Whole Numbers

When you read a word problem, certain <u>questions</u> can help you determine how to correctly solve the problem.

**Word problems: Do I multiply or divide?**

### <u>Multiplication</u>

- Is the problem asking for a total?
- Are you taking part of the total?
- Are you taking part of the part?
- Are you trying to determine a certain amount you need for something?

### <u>Division</u>

- Are you dividing a given amount into equal groups?
- Are you taking an amount and sorting it, breaking it up or cutting it into equal groups?
- Are you using an equal amount of a total and looking for how much used?

When you solve word problems using **COINS**, remember to read the problem, then solve it as follows:

**C**ircle: <u>Circle the key words and relevant information (and cross out any irrelevant information).</u>

**O**peration: : <u>**X**</u>, <u>**÷**</u>, etc.

**I**nformation: <u>Write the relevant information</u>.

**N**umber Sentence: <u>Write the math problem</u>.

**S**olution Sentence: <u>Write the solution as a full sentence</u>.

# Complete the Problems

Use the **COINS Strategy** to solve these advanced fraction word problems. Remember to circle the key words, draw pictures if necessary, and cross out any extra information. Then complete the steps in **COINS Strategy**.

**1.** A water supplier ships 47 cans of water per hour on an average workday. If there are 8 hours in the day, how many cans of water are shipped out daily?

❑ Circle key words & relevant information.

Operation: _____

Information: _____

_____

Number Sentence: _____

Solution Sentence: _____

_____

work space

**2.** A theme park takes up 5,688 acres. If the park is split into 4 equal areas, how many acres does each area comprise?

❑ Circle key words & relevant information.

Operation: _____

Information: _____

_____

Number Sentence: _____

Solution Sentence: _____

_____

work space

**3.** Sophia makes teapots and charges $36 for each one. If she sells an average of 108 teapots per day, how much money does she make a week?

❏ Circle key words & relevant information.

Operation: _____

Information: _____

_____

Number Sentence: _____

Solution Sentence: _____

_____

work space

**4.** A large hotel in California has a total of 1,764 rooms over 14 floors. How many rooms are on each floor?

❏ Circle key words & relevant information.

Operation: _____

Information: _____

_____

Number Sentence: _____

Solution Sentence: _____

_____

work space

**5.** A meat factory pays each worker $304.81 per day. If there are 105 workers, how much do they pay their workers in total each day?

❏ Circle key words & relevant information.

Operation: _____

Information: _____

_____

Number Sentence: _____

Solution Sentence: _____

_____

work space

**6.** A warehouse ship 355 boxes of soda per day. If each box holds 42 cans of soda, how many cans of soda are shipped out each day?

❏ Circle key words & relevant information.

Operation: _____

Information: _____

_____

Number Sentence: _____

Solution Sentence: _____

_____

work space

**7.** Mike won $95,778 on a scratch card. He wants to give his three children half of his winnings, split equally among them. How much will each child receive?

❑ Circle key words & relevant information.

Operation: _____

Information: _____

_____

Number Sentence: _____

Solution Sentence: _____

_____

work space

**8 .** A package delivery company delivered 8,368 packages in 16 days. If they delivered the same amount of packages each day, how many packages were delivered in a day?

❑ Circle key words & relevant information.

Operation: _____

Information: _____

_____

Number Sentence: _____

Solution Sentence: _____

_____

work space

**9.** Mrs. Ford spend $1,546 a year for daycare for her twin girls. How much does she spend for three years of daycare?

❑ Circle key words & relevant information.

Operation: _____

Information: _____

_____

Number Sentence: _____

Solution Sentence: _____

_____

work space

**10.** A parking lot in New York city made $5,535 on a Saturday night. If they charged each car $27 for parking, how many car parked in the lot that night?

❑ Circle key words & relevant information.

Operation: _____

Information: _____

_____

Number Sentence: _____

Solution Sentence: _____

_____

work space

**11.** If an average person blinks 28,800 times per day, how many times do they blink in a week?

❑ Circle key words & relevant information.

Operation: _____

Information: _____

_____

Number Sentence: _____

Solution Sentence: _____

_____

work space

**12 .** Becky went to a doctor twice each month every month in the year 2021. If she spent $1,512 on medical fees that year and each doctor charged the same amount, how much did each appointment cost?

❑ Circle key words & relevant information.

Operation: _____

Information: _____

_____

Number Sentence: _____

Solution Sentence: _____

_____

work space

**13.** A farmer plated 156 rows of corn with 60 bushels of corn in each row. How many bushels of corn did she plant in all?

❏ Circle key words & relevant information.

Operation: _____

Information: _____

_____

Number Sentence: _____

Solution Sentence: _____

_____

work space

**14.** A New York City library has 13,914 books organized on racks with 6 books per rack. How many racks are necessary to hold every book?

❏ Circle key words & relevant information.

Operation: _____

Information: _____

_____

Number Sentence: _____

Solution Sentence: _____

_____

work space

**15.** The population of a town was 13,459 in 1975. By the year 2022, the population had increased by 15 times. What was the population in 2022?

❑ Circle key words & relevant information.
_____

Operation: _____

Information: _____

_____

Number Sentence: _____

Solution Sentence: _____

_____

work space

**16 .** A total of 2,785 students competed in a cheerleading competition. If each team had 15 students, how many teams were there altogether?

❑ Circle key words & relevant information.

Operation: _____

Information: _____

_____

Number Sentence: _____

Solution Sentence: _____

_____

work space

**17.** Isabella bought 41 concert tickets for her and her classmates. If she paid $3690 in total, how much did each concert ticket cost?

❏ Circle key words & relevant information.

Operation: _____

Information: _____

_____

Number Sentence: _____

Solution Sentence: _____

_____

work space

**18 .** Liam reads an average of 205 words per minute. How many words can he read in 12 hours?

❏ Circle key words & relevant information.

Operation: _____

Information: _____

_____

Number Sentence: _____

Solution Sentence: _____

_____

work space

**19.** Mia traveled 720 miles and needed to stop to fuel up 5 times. If she fueled up each time the tank was empty, how many miles could she travel on a full tank of gas?

❑ Circle key words & relevant information.

Operation: _____

Information: _____

_____

Number Sentence: _____

Solution Sentence: _____

_____

work space

**20.** At a wedding there are 35 tables with 8 people sitting at each table. If each guest receives three plates for the food being served, how many plates are laid out in total?

❑ Circle key words & relevant information.

Operation: _____

Information: _____

_____

Number Sentence: _____

Solution Sentence: _____

_____

work space